Scenic | FERNIE
BRITISH COLUMBIA

A CANADIAN ROCKIES TREASURE IN PHOTOGRAPHS

Photography by Mark Gallup, Gerry George, Henry Georgi and Terry Parker

Written by Bethan Hull

SAVAGE PUBLISHING

SAVAGE
PUBLISHING

Copyright © 2001 by Savage Publishing

Published by
Savage Publishing
PO Box 2025
Fernie, BC, Canada, V0B 1M0
www.SavagePublishing.com

Dan Savage, Publisher
Bethan Hull, Editor
Samantha Walsh, Graphic Designer
Nicole Moore, Comptroller

Printed in Canada by Tri•Ad Press Ltd., Calgary, AB
www.TriadPress.com

National Library of Canada Cataloguing in Publication Data

Hull, Bethan, 1976-
  Scenic Fernie, British Columbia

  ISBN 0-9689780-0-2
  1. Fernie (B.C.)--Pictorial works. I. Gallup, Mark. II. Title.
FC3849.F4H82 2001   971.1'65   C2001-911466-4
F1089.5.F47H84 2001

Gerry George

Cover Photo: Grass and reeds in the flatlands on the banks of the Elk River sing out in autumn colour, with Mount Fernie, the Three Sisters and Mount Proctor reflected in the crystalline waters. Photo by Gerry George

Back Cover Photo: The Lizard Range is cast in a warm red light at dawn.
Photo by Henry Georgi

Page i: A peak in the north end of the Lizard Range is illuminated in a frosty winter glow.

Page ii-iii: A ski-tourer climbs to Thunder Meadows backcountry cabin.

Above Left: A lone larch tree in a pine and fir stand.

Savage Publishing gratefully acknowledges the following companies for making major contributions to *Scenic Fernie*.

Their support truly exemplifies great community spirit. For their efforts to enrich the community they serve, Savage Publishing thanks

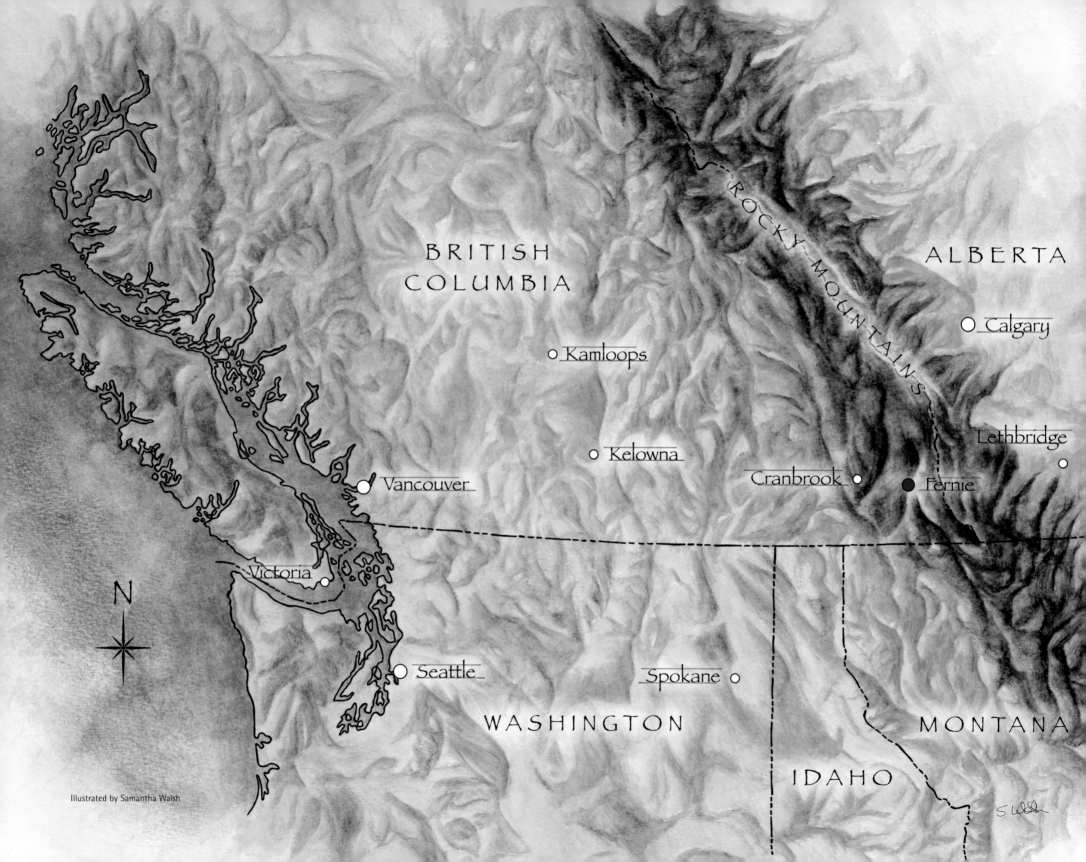

BRITISH
COLUMBIA

ROCKY MOUNTAINS

ALBERTA

○ Calgary

○ Kamloops

Lethbridge

○ Kelowna

Cranbrook ○ ● Fernie

○ Vancouver

Victoria

N

Seattle ○ Spokane ○

WASHINGTON

IDAHO

MONTANA

Illustrated by Samantha Walsh

S. Walsh

Right: The Elk River flows past

the Fernie Golf and Country

Club and on through the city to

Fernie Alpine Resort in this

aerial view of the valley.

Henry Georgi

Gerry George

Above: In winter, the snowy north end

of the Lizard Range catches the initial

rays of the rising sun.

INTRODUCTION

Nestled deep in the southeastern corner of British Columbia, cradled in the spectacular western edge of the

Canadian Rocky Mountains and nourished by the picturesque Elk River, Fernie is a scenic wonder. From the

undulating landscape of peaks and ridges of the surrounding mountains, to the neighbouring valleys, lakes

and farmland, Fernie is situated amid some of the most majestic and inspiring vistas in the world.

Above: Fernie Mountain looms over a dirt road with the city of Fernie sprawling behind the trees in this 1920's photograph.

Fernie takes its name from William Fernie, who along with Colonel James Baker were the main players in the drive to bring coal mining to the valley. It took ten years to raise enough money to build the mines and the railway needed to transport the coal to market. In 1897 coal mining began in the region and in 1898 the Canadian Pacific Railroad arrived, and with it, the town of Fernie. As Fernie grew, logging quickly became the second largest industry in the area with logging camps employing hundreds of men.

Just over a century ago, populated seasonally by First Nations peoples, Fernie was a pristine wilderness. The region remained relatively untouched until the exploration of the Crowsnest Pass in 1873 by Michael Phillips. This discovery, and the sighting of outcroppings of coal, opened the region to the rest of the continent.

Above: The Lizard Range is barren following the fires at the turn of the century.

Right: The Lizard Range, home of Fernie Alpine Resort and Island Lake Lodge, is a dramatic backdrop for historic downtown Fernie. The buildings, made primarily of brick and stone, are a legacy of those who settled this rugged valley despite the many hardships they faced.

Although Fernie's is a short history, it is one plagued by natural and human disasters. Mining accidents ravaged the region from Fernie to the eastern entrance of the Crowsnest Pass in the early days of mining, claiming numerous lives. Fire reduced Fernie's primarily wooden commercial district to smoldering rubble in April 1904. In August 1908 a second devastating fire gutted the entire city. The townsfolk literally ran for their lives and in less than 90 minutes the town was reduced to ashes.

Henry Georgi

The residents were undeterred and by 1910 Fernie was rebuilt: this time in brick and stone. The population soared to 6,000 and Fernie flourished into a thriving city, guided by the unwavering resolve and determination of its residents. These fires, more than any other, shaped the physical appearance of Fernie to this day as is seen in the brick and stone buildings that beautify downtown Fernie.

Gerry George

Many lightheartedly attribute the unfortunate history of the city to a curse that hangs over the valley. On a summer evening, out of Mount Hosmer's south face comes the Ghostrider: the darkened shadow of a distinctive horse and rider who some say is an angry Indian chief and his daughter pursuing William Fernie (left). As legend tells it, William was betrothed to an Indian Princess in order to learn the source of her coal bead necklace. After learning the location of the Morrissey Coal Seams he left the Princess. In revenge, the tribe's medicine woman placed a curse on the Elk Valley.

Although discounted by many, the misfortune of the region is often reason enough to believe. It makes for a fascinating tale, especially considering the many tragedies in Fernie's past.

In 1964 members of the Kootenay Tribes assembled in Fernie and performed a curse lifting ceremony, smoking a pipe of peace with local politicians. Still the legend lives on in the shadow on the mountain and in the stories of the townspeople.

Left: Housed in a relocated fully restored Canadian Pacific Railway Station, The Arts Station is a performing and fine arts venue with gallery, café, theatre and art studios. The relocation and restoration projects were a community volunteer effort.

Henry Georgi

Right: Built in the Edwardian Chateau Style, the Fernie Courthouse is a landmark, often considered the most beautiful in British Columbia.

Fernie's troubled history continued on into the depression of the thirties, when the city was brought to its knees and population and prosperity were reduced. Government subsidies kept the stagnant coal industry alive until the 1960s when it was revitalized by world coal markets. Today coal remains a pillar of Fernie's economy.

In 1963 locally owned Fernie Snow Valley opened, laying the foundation for today's resort by cutting runs and building lifts. Years later, the first on-mountain subdivision was built.

Henry Georgi

Fuelled by enthusiastic residents, Fernie bid for the 1968 Winter Olympics and the region took its first steps in becoming a world-class resort. In 1998 the resort was sold and was renamed Fernie Alpine Resort. The ski area was doubled with the construction of new lifts and building began in earnest on the alpine village at the base of the resort.

Set against the backdrop of the impressive spine of the Lizard Range, and flanked by the rugged peaks of the Three Sisters and Hosmer Mountains, Fernie truly is a Rocky Mountain treasure.

Henry Georgi

Above: In the foreground of Hosmer Mountain a field of golden dandelions basks in the summer sun.

Boasting phenomenal skiing, snowboarding, snowmobiling, fishing, mountain biking, golfing, rafting, paddling and hiking, this alpine community plays host to the world's adventurers and nature lovers.

In winter Fernie is blanketed by an abundance of powder. Trapped by the high ridgeline of the Lizard Range, storm systems often remain in Fernie for days. Still relatively unknown compared to other resort destinations, Fernie Alpine Resort is one of the best-kept secrets in North America. Also perched on the Lizard Range is Island Lake Lodge on the bank of Island Lake, a world-renowned snow-cat resort.

Phenomenal winter recreation has put Fernie on the map, but in the springtime, Fernie truly comes alive. Draped in a lush green velvet of the forest that spans the entire region and speckled with wildflowers and pristine springs, Fernie is at its best.

Fernie Golf and Country Club, Fernie Alpine Resort and Island Lake Lodge draw thousands of visitors each summer, steadily making Fernie a popular year-round destination. These summer visitors are discovering the mountain lifestyle the locals have always enjoyed.

The people who make this lush river valley their home, who face the challenging task of shaping its future, define the true character of Fernie.

Scenic Fernie celebrates the natural magnificence of the region's mountains, forests, rivers and lakes, and is a tribute to the people who make this lush river valley their home.

In spring and summer the mountains come alive in bold colour, vibrantly rejuvenated after a long winter with a bright carpet of wildflowers, grasses and deciduous trees over the mountainsides. Snowpack meltwater and rainfall ensure the Fernie area remains beautiful throughout the warmer seasons.

Left: This sub-alpine meadow is strewn with fragrant wildflowers; a treat for the intrepid hiker.

Henry Georgi

Mark Gallup

Facing Page: A common inhabitant of the Fernie area, bears command a healthy respect. This black bear is contentedly lounging in the first light of dawn.

Above: Caught in a ray of light, these flowers turn their heads towards the sun.

Terry Parker

Facing Page: Well on their way before the fog has lifted from the valley floor, a family takes advantage of the cooler morning temperatures to enjoy one of the many hikes in the area.

Dan Savage

Terry Parker

Common species to the area are bighorn sheep (above) and mountain goats (right).

Terry Parker

Above: The snowy peaks of Fernie Alpine Resort in early summer are reflected brightly in the lush carpet of daisies at the resort's base. Home to a phenomenal network of alpine and sub-alpine trails and spectacular views, Fernie Alpine Resort is steadily becoming a year-round resort destination.

Gerry George

Above: The village at the base of Fernie Alpine Resort is home to a wide selection of shops and services, including the four star Lizard Creek Lodge, which offers distinctive accommodation, dining and spa facilities.

Facing Page: Currie Bowl at Fernie Alpine Resort is extraordinary in both summer and winter, offering varied terrain for the adventurer throughout the year. The area is easily accessed from the chairlifts, which run in summer months for mountain bikers, hikers, and those looking for amazing views.

Terry Parker

The clear emerald waters of Lower

Silver Springs Lake are alive with

colour and texture in autumn.

Popular in the summer months for

the cool refreshing water, the chain

of lakes is frequented by swimmers

and cliff-jumpers.

Henry Georgi

Gerry George

The dense thicket of mossy undergrowth parts for a fresh mountain stream (right), while an old miner's shack is reclaimed by the forest (below).

Gerry George

The forests surrounding Fernie are predominantly young lodgepole pine and larch stands that regenerated after the great fires of the early 1900s. Small pockets of old growth cedar were spared in the valley and along the Lizard Range, creating an ecosystem unique to the area.

Facing Page: Hosmer Mountain is the site of the Ghostrider legend (see page 6), and is also a popular physically demanding hike.

Mark Gallup

Gerry George

Facing Page: Beauty surrounds this group of golfers at The Fernie Golf and Country Club, a championship course that opened in 1918.

Above: Speckled with brightly hued larch trees in early autumn, the dyke walk is as picturesque as it is peaceful. This popular walk weaves through the city on the banks of the Elk River and Coal Creek.

Right: Mid-afternoon sunlight dapples the leaves on this stand of aspen trees.

Gerry George

Henry Georgi

Facing Page: Nestled high on the Lizard Range, on the shores of Island Lake amid mountainous forested terrain, is Island Lake Lodge. A world-class four-season resort, Island Lake Lodge is known in the summer for hiking and mountain biking, and in winter for cat-skiing.

Terry Parker

Left: A small island of yellow grass breaks the perfect symmetry of this scene at Island Lake.

Below: A bald eagle rests on a nearby tree.

Henry Georgi

Terry Parker

The mountainous terrain surrounding Fernie makes it a popular mountain biking destination. Single-track and old logging roads tame the mountain peaks and valley floor with an impressive network of biking trails.

Left: Hoodoo spires stand as sentries over the flats of the Elk River near the BC-Montana border in a region known by locals as the South Country.

The South Country , which is 20 minutes from Fernie, seems to be a different land altogether, known for arid grasslands and dry weather. Fernie, by contrast, is one of the wettest regions west of the Pacific Coast due to the Lizard Range's ridgeline that traps storm systems crossing the Washington Plateau.

24

Facing Page: The sunlit ridgeline at Fernie Alpine Resort weaves an exposed trail to Polar Peak. It is one of the most scenic trails in the area.

Cross-country riders explore the single-track above the Ridgemont subdivision (right). Silhouetted in the waning light, a mountain biker enjoys the final ride of the day (far right). Bikers drive up the winding Cedar Valley Road to Island Lake Lodge (lower right).

Terry Parker

Gerry George

Mark Gallup

Henry Georgi

Gerry George

Facing Page: Daisies seem to spray from this rider's spokes at the base of Proctor Mountain.

Left: Caged in by the lodgepole pine forest, a biker rides into a patch of sunlight on a trail at the base of Castle Mountain.

Above: A ghostly white trail is left by a biker speeding down a trail on Fernie Mountain.

Henry Georgi

29

With hundreds of rivers and streams in the area and an abundance of trout, fishing in Fernie is spectacular.

Henry Georgi

Facing Page: The fishing line dances in mid-afternoon light at Silver Springs Lake.

Above: Guided fishing excursions include drift boat rides on the Elk River: a winding float through beautiful country.

Left: Early morning fog rises at the river's edge as a fly fisher casts his line on the Elk River.

Henry Georgi

Henry Georgi

Rafters challenge the whitewater rapids of the Lower Elk River south of Fernie (far left). From above, the rafters look tiny next to the deep canyon walls towering over them (left).

Gerry George

Above: Overlooking Lake Koocanusa, a climber scales a

seemingly smooth rockface.

Henry Georgi

Facing Page: Turquoise water

contrasts brightly with the red

and yellow hulls of kayaks at Lake

Koocanusa, a 145-kilometre long

lake created with the damming of

the Kootenay River. It's a popular

summer spot for swimming and

boating with sandy beaches and

warm calm water.

Left: Cumulus clouds darken

the waters ahead of canoeists

at Silver Springs Lake.

Henry Georgi

Henry Georgi

Fernie is home to a large and active river kayaking community.

Melting snowpack and spring rain provide great paddling from

early spring to late summer on the Elk, Wigwam and Bull Rivers.

Henry Georgi

The Elk River from Hosmer to Fernie Alpine

Resort is a scenic run perfect for beginners

and spring training. The Ghostrider Wave, in

Fernie, is a popular place to surf (above).

The 15-metre Elk River Falls is a spectacular

sight (left). A daring kayaker runs the falls at

medium flow (facing page).

Dan Savage

Autumn in Fernie is an intense flash of colour across the mountain slopes and over the valley floor before

the snow begins to fall in late October and early November.

Gerry George

Facing Page: Surrounded by glorious fall foliage, this moose feeds in the warm autumn sun.

Left: The city of Fernie is alight in the emerald glow of aurora borealis, the northern lights.

Right: An annual event in Fernie is the Mogul Smoker. Skiers and snowboarders sacrifice old equipment

to the Griz, a mythical mountain man who is said to be responsible for the region's epic snowfall.

Started about a quarter century ago by skiers, the Mogul Smoker is a Fernie tradition.

Following Page: Ablaze in a vibrant alpine glow, the Lizard Range at sunrise is magnificent.

Mark Gallup

Henry Georgi

Terry Parker

Facing Page: Elusive creatures of the backcountry, cougars are rarely seen,

although paw prints in the snow are a common sight.

Terry Parker

Right: Elk abound in the Fernie area. Reflected in the calm waters, an elk pauses

in the frosted grass.

Above: Howling can often be heard from populations of coyotes and wolves. This

timber wolf pauses in a snowy clearing at the outskirts of Fernie Alpine Resort.

Terry Parker

In winter the Lizard Range receives an impressive 850 centimetres of snowfall, dramatically changing the area's mountains. Under a blanket of snow, the region is almost unrecognizable from the bare rockfaces and ridgelines that dominate the landscape in summer and fall.

This Page: A much different landscape in summer (above), a snowboarder soars through the air in front of a steep ridgeline at Island Lake Lodge (right).

Facing Page: Over a once rocky knoll (right), a snowboarder carves past an impressive rock face (left).

Mark Gallup

Mark Gallup

44

Henry Georgi

The pristine mountainous terrain surrounding Fernie offers backcountry travelers a spectacular world to explore, although avalanches are always a risk. In the stark whiteness of snow and cloud, a colourful sun dog frames this group of skiers (right).

Gerry George

Above: A tree casts a shadow over snow battered by sun, wind and rain late in late spring.

Henry Georgi

Henry Georgi

Above: A group of ski-tourers access the mountains near Fernie at their own speed, taking advantage of the peace and tranquility to enjoy the view.

Facing Page: Snowmobiling opens up the backcountry, offering easy access and a thrilling ride.

46

Island Lake lodge is the best-known

cat-skiing operation in the world,

offering skiers and snowboarders an

endless supply of untracked powder.

Right: The Three Bears, the smaller

peaks in the foreground, are

illuminated in a sublime purple

glow at dawn.

Gerry George

Henry Georgi

Facing Page: Misty clouds sing with light as they wrap around a nearby peak at Island Lake Lodge; a skier takes in the beauty surrounding her.

Henry Georgi

Above: Steep chutes and couloirs tower over a group of skiers and snowboarders as they prepare for a day of powder and sunshine at Island Lake Lodge.

Left: Picturesque Island Lake reflects the towering Lizard Range as frost plays on blades of grass at the shore.

Mark Gallup

Henry Georgi

Fernie Alpine Resort is a welcome escape

from over-crowded mega-resorts. With

diverse terrain for all levels of skier and

snowboarder, limitless tree skiing, vast

bowls and steep chutes, Fernie Alpine

Resort ranks among the top resorts in

North America.

Left: A skier in Timber Bowl

enjoys what Fernie is known

for: an abundance of powder.

Below: A skier cruises down a

steep run.

Henry Georgi

Facing Page: The Elk River winds its way

parallel with the base of Fernie Alpine

Resort in early morning.

Mark Gallup

52

Facing Page: An example of classic Rocky Mountain Canadian

architecture, Olympic gold medallist Kerrin Lee-Gartner's

Snow Creek Lodge rests on the slopes at Fernie Alpine Resort.

Right and Below: A bustling alpine village, Fernie Alpine Resort

is beautifully scenic.

Henry Georgi

Gerry George

Henry Georgi

Kerrin Lee Gartner's
SNOW CREEK LODGE

Mark Gallup

A trail of snow fuses with the

clouds in the sky on a typical

day of bottomless powder at

Island Lake Lodge.

Mark Gallup

Facing Page: A fiery stream of snow

dances in the fading light behind this

snowboarder in the backcountry.

Mark Gallup

Mark Gallup

Left: Leaning into a deep carve at Island Lake Lodge, a rooster tail of powder fans into the air.

Above: A snowboarder sends up a torrent of snow, brightly lit by the late afternoon sun.

Henry Georgi

Henry Georgi

Above: Almost entirely hidden by snow, a skier surfs through deep powder.

Left: Bulbous gargoyles of snow border a ridgeline at Fernie Alpine Resort as a skier descends Polar Peak.

Facing Page: Luminous clouds feather the sky as a skier tucks and launches off a cliff in the backcountry near Fernie.

Mark Gallup

Henry Georgi

Mark Gallup

Facing Page: Fernie lies silent under a thick blanket of cloud.

Hosmer, Three Sisters, Proctor and Fernie Mountains rear their

snowcapped peaks out of the clouds as a group of

snowboarders looks on.

Right: Cast in the blue glow of winter, the undulating peaks of

the Rocky Mountains hide under cloud cover at the horizon as a

skier descends Polar Peak at Fernie Alpine Resort. The White Pass

Quad chairlift awaits on the ridgeline.

Above: Steep and deep—snowboarders descend a chute at

Island Lake Lodge.

Henry Georgi

Capturing an inversion at Fernie
Alpine Resort, coloured spheres
of light play in the camera's lens.
Below the fog the valley is in
shadow, while above the sun
shines in clear blue skies.

Gerry George

Mark Gallup

Left: A backcountry skier and his dog stop above Fernie Alpine Resort to enjoy the fading sunset.

Facing Page and Right: Crisp mountain weather and bluebird skies create an irresistible climate for the winter adventurer. The snow-covered golf course and trails surrounding Fernie Alpine Resort offer unbeatable cross-country skiing and snowshoeing.

Mark Gallup